Renou

Rela

Repeat

A Poetic Journey Down the Dark Road of

Alcohol Addiction and Recovery

By Conor Richardson

Table of Contents

Dedication

To my family, especially Lisa my rock. I put you all through so much.

Acknowledgments

Without my family, in particular, my wife supporting me through my numerous attempts, I would have failed. Without the understanding of my employer and, in doing so, giving me something to aim for, again, I would have failed. Another reason for not failing was the excellent guidance and practical advice and exercises I received from my Cognitive Behavioural Therapist. When you are talking about alcoholism, failure ultimately means death, so in truth, I wouldn't be here without you.

About the Author

Conor Richardson was born in Dublin, Ireland and spent his formative years in Chapelizod a village on the outskirts with the Phoenix Park as his garden. He is happily married with 3 children and one dog. This is his first publication but has been writing on and off for over 20 years.

Introduction

I had reached the stage in my life where I wasn't dealing with my problems, be they small, medium or large. Looking back, the large ones were a handful, but proper thinking could have been dealt with. I have all the same problems now, but I don't have any large ones. A contradiction? No, it's not. The problems that seemed large back then are now small and easily dealt with.

Problems meant anxiety for me. Not dealing with them led to intolerable anxiety, which in turn led me to depend on alcohol. I don't see the benefit in over-analysing my early years to try and find a reason why I was too weak to deal with my problems. I will say one thing, low self-esteem and alcohol are an extremely dangerous combination.

I went as low as I thought I could go with alcohol but still managed to find a lot of new pits to fall into.

At the time of writing this introduction, I am many years in recovery. The following poems/thoughts were written at various stages of my addiction and numerous recovery attempts. They are quite personal, but I feel that people considering quitting or in recovery have many similar experiences, so some of the poems may strike a chord with many readers.

Existence is littered with obstacles, both mental and physical, but are they really in your way or has your anxiety placed them there? This brings to my mind an old Irish saying "Don't break your shin on a stool that's not in your way".

The human mind is incredibly powerful, but it can become a tool of your own destruction. Think of it like a computer where negative thoughts are a virus which can cause massive damage and impact how you think, feel and behave. What I needed to do to overcome my alcohol addiction was construct a kind of firewall around my mind which filtered out the destructive thoughts.

Cognitive Behavioural Therapy (CBT) sessions with an excellent therapist started this process, but without the support of my family and my workplace, I would not have even taken that step. The first issue was to identify the negative thoughts, and that is where this collection of poems came in. My mind was a jumble of hazy conflicting thoughts, but the act of writing and trying to discover rhyming words was essential in defining my feelings and isolating individual thoughts. Many of the poems are quite short as they have completed their purpose.

The first poem, Downhill, was ironically written many years before the drink took a stranglehold on my life, but you can see that even then, I had a pretty bleak outlook. Although it hadn't taken a stranglehold at that point, there were still some signs which I should have noticed.

Included throughout the book is a selection of Sobering Thoughts, which, as the name suggests, are insights I had during my recovery which may provide some assistance in achieving sobriety.

The Poems

Downhill

Long-gone wide-eyed innocence

Replaced with cynical common sense

What was a diamond is a rhinestone,

A dream a millstone

Round my neck as I decline

Into a world that once could be mine.

Just the One

Just the one will wash my defences away,

Break down the barriers that keep my demon at bay.

Just the one will tear my motivation from me,

Cut deep into the heart of my family.

Just the one will make me an empty shell,

Barren inside, lonely on the outside as well.

Just the one will kill me next time round,

Push me through the earth to six feet underground.

Just the one is a game of Russian roulette,

With every chamber loaded, there is only death.

Just the one,

Can't be done.

Ever.

Sobering Thought 1

I used to find myself confused when I heard the expression "the next drink will kill you". I pictured somebody taking a sip of alcohol and keeling over dead. I came to realise that one drink would mean you were back in the alcohol pit and would most likely not get another chance at recovery.

Get Back Up

I will never get back up again
One more bottle and I will be lost
In a world where I will die in pain
Take a drink; you know the cost

No more strength for another play.
Temptation will show its face to me
If I give in, prepare my grave today,
Flesh to dust for all eternity

Have a drink, have it your way
Don't get back up; live selfishly.
For me to have a future at all
A life worth living with family
I cannot allow even one more fall
Stay up this time, permanently
One more drink will end it all

Find a Direction

The road I'm on may be the safe way

It might keep me away from drinking today

But it can't sustain me totally

There is more to life than staying alcohol-free

I need to pave the road with things for me

I will find a direction that works for all

Complacency will lead to my final fall

A future will be put into place

With plans, goals and challenges to face

Let the past fade without a trace

The past contains both good and bad

But the memories I retain are overwhelmingly sad.

I can proceed even on my own

I cannot leave until my confidence has grown

I am not there yet, but the seeds are sown

Rooms of My Mind

At night I pace the rooms of my mind

Looking for answers or questions of a different kind

In certain rooms, I cannot linger too long

I might find a harsh truth or a forgotten wrong

Some rooms have doors on every side

Other dark corners where bad memories hide.

Maybe I should go there and give them light

They are part of me, wrong or right

My mind will imprison me if I dwell there all day.

With the darkest rooms, there is a price to pay.

Sobering Thought 2

Lying in bed at night worrying, sound familiar? That was me, I would imagine the worst case scenario for the slightest anxiety in my mind. This became intolerable and was one of the reasons alcohol took hold. These days I allow myself 10 minutes maximum worrying time each night. It is really about applying the serenity prayer to these thoughts: accept what you cannot change (life is full of things outside of our control) and identify what you can change. Bed is not the place to change anything, just deciding that you will change something can greatly ease the associated anxiety.

Turns are Gone

I am what I have done and the way that I live
My time gone by has given all that it can give
The future will come to me with each rising sun
No looking back at the turns that have gone.

I have just existed too long, never filling each day
Time has been wasted, stolen; now it's time to pay
I don't want to be a train with tracks to stay on
I want choices now the old turns have gone.

Sometimes a thousand thoughts invade my brain
I can move them now to where they cause no pain
All my problems can now be analysed
Either to be cast aside or prioritised.

AA?

If I go, I will have to bring my mind

If I go, I will have to leave preconceptions behind

If I go, I will have to stay

AA? Not today.

When I got there, I would have to socialise

When I got there, I would see myself through others' eyes.

When I got there, I would leave straight away

AA? Not today.

If I stayed, I would deal with it all

I would listen to the drinkers' downfall

If I stayed, I would really hear what they say

AA? Maybe today.

Are darkened rooms all that I will find

Or is that just the image locked in my mind

I need people to listen to what I say

AA? OK.

Sobering Thought 3

The times I attended AA meetings did not work out for me as I was still harbouring ridiculous thoughts that I did not have a problem and just needed to cut back. For many people they are an essential part of recovery but I found the practical aspect of CBT to be of more benefit.

Time is Mine

The future is today; the future is the next few moments

Tomorrow is too far away, shrouded in uncertain events

Decisions taken too soon leave too much time to dwell

Today is now, and what's to come as well

Time is what and when I want it to be

A second can be a flash or eternity

Time is mine; every day is mine to use

Time is mine, and there isn't a moment to lose

Father

I am a father, biologically

I haven't been the best, the best I could truly be

Is it too late? Have I pushed them too far

Away from me and towards a lonely bar.

There is still time, time to right some wrongs

But some memories they will always take along.

The past is gone; I need to light the present now

Try and brighten their lives and fix it all somehow.

I can't always look for the easy life

Leaving all the tough decisions to my loving wife.

Excuses

I didn't want to write this; I might find it hard

I look for ways out of things that upset my routine

I can convince myself that I've played the right card

But I know deep down what I really mean.

Just because I wrote a poem doesn't mean the problem's solved

A thousand words or thoughts aren't any action at all

While my head's in the sand, the issues have evolved

It may be tough, but often confrontation is the right call.

Therapy

Thoughts are always in my head

Some constructed and some uninvited

They lead to feelings where dangerous seeds are planted

Where my wish for alcohol is granted.

Overthinking leads to anxiety

And leaves me with feelings of inadequacy

When I need to escape from the prison of my brain

I turn to my Kryptonite, the poison from the grain.

The path I found to lead me away, finally

Brought me reluctantly to Therapy

No instant success, I continued to fail

Would my coffin receive its final nail?

Sobering Thought 4

To operate a supercomputer with even a fraction of the power of the human brain would require extensive studying and training. There is no user manual for our mind and early education is focused on facts and formulas with no focus on how to deal with our thoughts. That is why I found CBT so beneficial as unlike counselling which primarily focuses on the past it provides practical advice and exercises to train your thoughts.

Temptation Calls

The time will come, left to my own devices
On my own to deal with my vices.
Strength and calmness will flow from my core
Time can be split, so it's not long anymore

I spend more than ever in solitude
With just my dog getting everything chewed
I am quite happy most of the time
Moments of malcontent aren't a crime

Temptation disguised as opportunity
Will come knocking and ask for me.
I will open the door and say, "Not today."
Keep to the path of my chosen way

Idle Hands

Poetry is my drug of choice today
But that won't always light my fire
Apathy is the danger of letting boredom have its way
I always need to have something to desire.

Idle hands are the devil's track
To an idle mind that's open to attack
There's often sunshine in the rain
Plans to be made, goals to attain.

All the world a stage, but I'm in the crowd
Watching from afar, interaction not allowed.
I need a part to play, a direction to follow
Not sitting on the bank watching the river flow

A Version of Blue

I'm living with a version of blue
Not quite sadness; more like I'm missing something
There is sunlight coming through
Erasing shadows makes me cleaner within

Issues unresolved cause ripples to spread
Affecting peaceful coves with disruptive force
Areas need to be sectioned within my head
For my life to go on a harmonious course

This version of blue fades in and out
I'm stranded between fractions of contented and deflated
I feel happy, but there's always some doubt
Sometimes the simplest thing makes me feel elated

Believed in Me

When my children don't reach their full potential

What I feel and believe is only incidental

I could have done more to motivate and inspire

I could have put a flame to their inner fire

Time has done little to take my guilt away

Time has given me a debt to pay

I need to be strong to help them now

And not be afraid, to be strong, somehow

The past is a prison that I've left behind

The future is a path I've yet to find.

When I reach the end, I've yet to see,

I want to be able to say

I BELIEVED IN ME

Fill the Void

If I dream of nothing, then nothing will come through

With my mind closed, I won't experience anything new

On my final day, I don't want regrets in my grave

I need to create memories and experiences to save

If I change nothing, I'll still only live in my head

And in the books, I read as I lie in my bed

I can convince myself that I flow with the tide

But there's a purpose missing, and a void inside

Sobering Thought 5

Routine is important in recovery. I was lucky, thanks to an understanding employer, that I still had a job to attend. I don't have a hectic social life but I find that I now find day to day activities more enjoyable. I now look forward to the weekends for the extra reading time at night. It may sound mundane but the social part of a social life disappeared years ago for me, it was all about the alcohol. I treated going out to dinner or the cinema as a waste of valuable drinking time.

Golden Day

Down the line, there will be a golden day

When it all comes together, I am at peace

But life doesn't work out that way

Death is the hour when my worries will cease.

Anxiety is a form of excitement, a thrill

A part of life that centres my aim

Life would be empty, a placebo pill

Give me stress every time over mundane.

Good and Selfish

Working on myself watching my family drown

If I don't fix myself, it will all come down

Cruel to be kind or whatever you call it

I am the foundation stone on which they all sit.

Selfish with a purpose, a mercenary with a plan

Being kind to myself so I will be all I can

I'll remove the blinkers and let them see it all

If I go Russian again everything will fall.

Sobering Thought 6

It was made abundantly clear to me on numerous occasions that my recovery would not succeed unless I was selfish. This may not seem fair to my family who had to put up with so much throughout my addiction. It is not fair but it has to be done. I needed to protect myself from situations that I saw as triggers and sometimes walk away when I was needed. The need for this selfishness lessened as my recovery progressed because I never stopped policing my thoughts.

Itchy Brain

I want something, even need

What it is, I can't explain

Itchy brain.

Thinking, maybe too much

Analysing, too close to the grain?

Itchy brain.

Feel relaxed, calm, and in control

Friends with Sandman again

But still… Itchy Brain.

Feelings bottled, hidden, ignored

Pushed away to avoid pain?

Itchy brain.

Sobering Thought 7

Sometimes you may feel on edge or anxious and be unable to identify why. I usually close my eyes for 5 minutes in a quiet room and quickly scan through my worries and also my to do list. I often discover something minor that I had forgotten to do. Even if you don't discover any cause I still find the search still removes or reduces the unidentified anxiety.

Cracked at Dawn

Anxious, apprehensive and agitated

Like I'm running late for the train

Is it early morning related?

My blood needs its addictions; it's vices again

Tension and strain are part of mornings tapestry

We both have reasons to want away

Early home pressure will weigh heavily

Responsibility stays at home on a work day.

Not flying straight as the black crow

Leaving the direct route leaves me with vague unease

An undercurrent unidentified unsettles me somehow

Returning to the route is like a refreshing breeze.

My Mind is Unique

I can't be sure anyone sees what I see

My perspective is shaped by events and my history,

Thoughts that burrow in and infest my brain

That cloud my mind turning sunshine into rain

To others would be a fleeting annoyance

They step back on the floor and continue the dance

My thoughts mutate and dictate my demeanour

Creating self-hate and consequential behaviour.

Sobering Thought 8

What is normal? You have lived with your own mind for your whole existence so your way of thinking is your normal. We all think differently and that is never going to change but this does not mean we should close our minds to learning new techniques.

Hidden from Me

There is something there that is evading me
A thing that taunts me just out of sight
It makes connections where there's none to see
Paranoia that makes me sure I'm right

Self-analysis can be a dangerous pursuit
Reflecting on imagined insecurity
It can be a seed that bears no fruit
Only weeds obscuring my reality

The doubts march back in on relapse day
I was sure they were gone permanently
They settle in like they were never away
From a place in my mind hidden from me.

Core

It's my nucleus formed at my core

Moulded by my experiences from day one

It's like ivy that will choke all before

Unless I tend it and keep it from the sun.

Adversity and opportunity are brothers

Set before me to challenge my placidity

If I swallow the fear that smothers

I can sculpt my own destiny

When I look now, I like what I see

The changes inside and the confidence I feel

I have grown away from crippling insecurity

Recognised my symptoms and challenged them to heal

Sobering Thought 9

Another thing I learned from therapy is that everyone has a core belief about themselves. Core beliefs are generally stable and resistant to change so if you have low self-esteem you will need to work against your belief about yourself.

Collateral Damage

If I could speak without fear, what would I say

Would I tell you that you're throwing your life away

Will I mention that you need to be strong

What can I say that you won't take up wrong

I could tell you it gets better with time

When you face your demons as I faced mine

I could tell you to grow up and raise your game

I can tell you because I was the same

Empathy is the last thing you need

Self-pity is where that road will lead

A road that's much longer when travelled alone

I need to show you the path from your comfort zone.

Dreamer Me and the Shadows

Time to make plans; the shadow has burnt away

Obscure notions real, Dreamer Me can have his say

Maybe the shade overshadowed the other lesser pains

They have come to the fore now the monster has been slain

My early years weren't an emotional festival

From my restricted view, it just seemed normal

Fewer friends equal fewer points of reference

But I look back now with some hindsight sense.

My memories are gone or hidden way below

Maybe my mind has an obliterating shadow

It could be that there is nothing to find

And Dreamer Me can leave the darkness behind

Fate has furnished me with a lucky break

Opened blocked paths, I now can take

It's not just luck; some of it's me

I kept up the fight and earned the victory

Rewind and Back

Clear the decks and leave regret in the past tense

Take the lessons learned, put them away for reference

I can rewind and observe, but I can't stay

A dispassionate study of when I took the wrong way.

When it must be done, but I can't do it instantly

I would let it grow into disabling anxiety

I can now redirect my thoughts to a better place

Still, I need more things to fill the better space.

Ideas collide and ricochet off to obscurity

Enthused for a moment, then rejected by cowardly me

Make a choice to advance with blinkers on

Or ignore the what-ifs and write my own song

Sobering Thought 10

Dwelling on things in the past is dangerous. Reminiscing is fine but thinking back on past mistakes (whether real or imagined) and berating yourself means you can't complete your recovery. Be nice to yourself, you deserve it because you are making changes.

Nobody is Superman

Others are or sometimes can be
Just as unsure or insecure as me
I have hazy goals and a vague plan
None require me to be Superman

Awareness of limitations shows me
Traps to avoid in adversity
Live for now but always prepare
The future is labelled "Handle with Care."

Paranoia Avenue

If I let my mind drift, I'll see the worst come through

It's all destined to happen; whatever I do

Have to keep my head away from Paranoia Avenue

Bad outcomes are endless; happy endings are few

Dangerous thoughts are louder, and blinker your view

Catastrophic thinking leads to Paranoia Avenue

Thoughts collide, negatives now far and few

Dawn is brighter, with no hint of blue

Far away from Paranoia Avenue

Sobering Thought 11

Throughout withdrawal and early recovery paranoia can take hold very quickly. This is addiction at work in your mind trying to engineer situations where you will feel justified in drinking again. Being aware of this can help to change your mind-set at these delicate stages.

Power Over Me

Maybe now I can enter the flames and emerge before I burn

Take my measure, taste the fire and know when to turn

The eyes blinded are mine, seeing what I want to see

I've broken some chains, but IT still has power over me.

Criticism swirls in my mind like distant laughter

It lives loud at the start but is buried soon after

I cling to vague memories of praise to preserve sobriety

I still hear it chant of its power over me

Horizon

There's nothing between me and my horizon

That's not good; it means my existence is flat

No adventures or excitement to depend on

Only possible pitfalls obscure my future path

Plans are the seeds of the experience

Anticipation, the stem where it's grown

The flower, the culmination of suspense

Without plans, the seeds are never sown.

Sobering Thought 12

Without plans your future can seem pointless sometimes, same things every day. This can lead to feelings of emptiness which your addiction will try to fill with desire for alcohol. Always try to have different activities, no matter how small pencilled in your diary.

Uncertainty

Uncertainty chips away at my defences and burrows deep inside

Leads me to seek false solidity behind which I can hide

I can't feel them, don't see them, but they notice me

Getting further and further away from the man I can be.

My escape options are limited with uncertainty in the air

I can open a book, but I'm too on edge to flee in there

Mindless games offer a welcome but far too brief respite

The chasm of temptation looms to pull me into an endless night.

Sobering Thought 13

I never liked uncertainty and not receiving concrete plans or answers would cause me anxiety and lead to my imagination heading down the darkest paths. This was dangerous during my recovery but now even though I still don't like it I don't allow my mind to over imagine anymore.

Premeditated Seclusion

Alone means no eyes judging me

Time to turn my thoughts internally

Try to make sense of my total dependence

Find a solution somehow that makes sense.

There is more out in the world

I just need my inner flag unfurled

Take the real me off the shelf

Just as soon as I find myself

Sobering Thought 14

Alone time is good but not too much. Your addiction drives people away but it is difficult to recover if you only have yourself to recover for. Try to be around people but make time to be alone with your thoughts.

Immovable

Temper collides with practised detachment resulting in cold silence,

It takes courage and strength before I traverse the gap.

The ice thaws gradually, the fire fades as we both see sense

As the days tick on, insecurity leads us back into its trap.

The immovable objectionable issue drives us relentlessly to the brink,

Easing up to fill us with a semblance of hope

When we ignore all memories and steadfastly refuse to think

Beyond a night, an hour, it's how we've learned to cope.

Motivation is fickle, broken by imagined catastrophes and foretold fails

Peace and quiet is a crossroads my mind can't find

I take a train of thought to a town and stay on the rails

But everything is too close to leave behind

Mundane, everyday sounds amplified by paranoia and fuelled by memory

Make everything quiet so you can hear what's not happening

Trying to connect, trying to communicate emotionally,

You try to impose your will, but apathy is their king.

Emotional Radar

I'm facing me, exhaustively scanning my inner ups and downs.

My moods are as well-known as my own home town.

Facing outwards is obscured with cloud and mist,

Emotions unrecognised; I often have to choose from a list.

What's affecting me is part of who I can be,

Ignorance of others leads me to anxious insecurity,

Second-guessing emotions, applying my own view

Reacting to signals that might not be true.

I can tell you're not yourself and know the reason why.

See and feel the tears but not fathom why you cry.

I need to feel your point of view, not hear or see.

Understand what it does to you and not how it affects me.

I need to see through your eyes and think with your brain

Walk for miles in your shoes until I feel your pain

I think of your burdens and how I would cope

It would end with me requesting the final rope

Sobering Thought 15

When you start abusing alcohol your emotional growth stops. You may find in the midst of your addiction and early recovery that you have difficulty reading people's emotions. My theory is that your addiction is making you see emotions in other people that will encourage you to drink.

Fate

You grow with them, do they know you
Shared the highs and frequent lows too
The past is a foundation on which we build
All the pockets of darkness can be filled

Nature or nurture is a pointless debate
We can change direction we're not tied to fate
The road of life is not one way
Our minds can repair our yesterday

Comfort dwells deep inside us all
We need to forgive ourselves and walk tall
The future is a paradise of choice
With the paths decided by your inner voice.

Buried But Not Dead

Far down now but still alive,
Waiting for any opportunity
It's the queen at the centre of my hive
Ready to rise and overwhelm me

It's only buried, not dead
Vaguely buzzing through my head
It won't even die with me
But live on in my victim's memories

I'm floating comfortably now
My head is well above the water
Life is calm from stern to bow
But I need to move to avoid slaughter

It's only buried, not dead
Vaguely swimming through my head
It won't even die with me
But live on in my victim's memories

I'm moving now and taking it slow
Feel like a horse and cart on a motorway
The rest are going too fast to have anywhere to go
I just take it day by day

Dark Thoughts

As the darkness comes and approaches, sleep
I write the lines in my head that I want to keep
If I leave that zone and ignite the light
I'll be chasing slumber through the night

I close my eyes and rest my mind
Leaving complicated thoughts behind
Words and phrases come along in time
With a little nudge rearranged to rhyme

They are moved immediately to the page
While they still reside in memories cage
For when morning comes, they will have fled
Leaving jumbled thoughts inside my head.

Assertive Balancing

When I take no crap from inside my mind

After I leave inner turmoil behind

I can begin to focus elsewhere

And deal with the issues out there

I don't assert myself in certain cases

So then overdo it in other places

It won't work when it's averaged out

To make up for all my own self-doubt

Unbalanced assertion makes me two different men

One slashes a sword the other wields a pen

I coax analytical thoughts down onto the page

Whilst out on the road, I unleash my rage

Meditate to Medicate

Opportunities lost,

wires crossed

When inside your head

is as heavy as lead

Turn your spotlight out,

your focus about

Meditate to medicate

Sobering Thought 16

Meditation is an essential tool in your recovery and is an excellent way of tuning you out from everything. Like a computer that starts running slowly needs a restart your brain too needs this. Sleep normally performs this function but if you are in the middle of a hectic day then meditation for 10-15 minutes can achieve the same result.

Adaptable Ambitions

No specific goals, no exact targets set

My friends are people I haven't met

Traveling a level path with no peaks or troughs to see

Adaptable ambitions keep leading back to me.

Starting hobbies and fads is my distraction

Which youthfully expire due to no conviction

Like a magpie distracted by a shiny detail

I move on quickly before I fail.

Vagrant Thoughts

Vagrant thoughts, loitering, begging to be fed
Traverse the hidden back streets in my head
Infrequently visiting the now well-lit thoroughfare
To accost the well-adjusted residing there

Intrusive thoughts, nagging, sending messages out
Convincing me I know what you're thinking about
Distracting, impacting on relaxing my mind
Diluted paranoia makes peace hard to find.

Spent Life

I want it because that is what I want to need

Make a choice between the flower and the weed

Desires exceed whatever you may own

In infant clay, the seed of greed was sown.

Just getting by is not accepted anymore

Accumulate until you sweat from every pore

Quiet time unheard, rest and peace lie dead

Dusty books, all the pages left unread.

A bird in a glass cage believes itself to be free

A depressed mind is black with no escape to see

Hellfire is the light at the end of a downward tunnel path

You can spend your life escaping internal wrath.

Spend your life completely with nothing left behind

The ones after you have their own way to find

Do what you want, forget the fear inside

Regret is a sin if you never even tried

Escape?

Heading to the sun, leaving darkness behind

Will the light penetrate the shadows in my mind?

Physical triggers are littered where I've been

If they travel in my mind remains to be seen

Will the sun, sea, and sights that I find

Be enough to distract my fragile mind

Will the late nights chip away at my willpower

And return me screaming to my darkest hour.

My Rock

Through too few highs and massive lows,
You've been there for me.
Since that distant day when we took our vows
You've been there for me.

There were crazy storms and dark skies,
many tears in a pool of lies that threatened to capsize
our fragile ship but despite my efforts to destabilize,
we've made it here because love survives.

When the bottle drained and the well was dry
You've been there for me.
When the pain was enough to make you cry
You've been there for me.

Countless empty promises and broken dreams,
false tears in drunken screams
stretching our bond at the seams,
you guided us through the treacherous streams.

When the smiles faded from our children's faces
You've been there for me.

When my mind was off in hallucinated places

You've been there for me.

False blame thrown at you and your family,

you suffered for my insecurity,

you took it all with dignity

to give us all stability

when the easy way was to break free.

When I forced your hand, and the police arrived

You've been there for me.

When I passed out, chaos thrived

You've been there for me.

Not Me Anymore

My eyes light up momentarily
Buoyed by the thought of inebriated festivity
Staggering home, a struggle to open the door
Spinning rooms, waking up on the floor
That's not me, Not Me Anymore

Days best forgotten, nights not recalled
Love, work, family, everything stalled
Work was a hassle, an unavoidable bore
Counting the minutes till twenty past four
That's not me, Not Me Anymore

Family ignored and pushed away
Couldn't talk to them or hear what they say
Completely blanked what happened before
But the guilt was twined through my core
That's not me, Not Me Anymore

Tried to drown in a forty-proof sea
Shunned the help that was thrown at me
Bottle after bottle till my soul was 1 sore
My throat bleeding as 1 screamed for more

That's not me, Not Me Anymore

I've closed the door to before

Not Me Anymore.

Temptations Name

A perpetual quest for personal growth

An endless drive for inner peace

It's me before family, but it can be both

The strive for balance will never cease

I've seen Hell and watched it pass

Those close to me seared by its flame

I do look back through toughened glass

But temptation no longer knows my name

Hope Filled Head

When shame was the main tenant in my brain
I stayed outside to avoid the pain
When anxiety called, I had no place to go
Only the end of a bottle and vodka's limbo

Solitude now has pleasant paths I can take
I follow these now for my sanity's sake
Where the footing is sure, and I don't stress
About meeting myself with sins to confess

My thoughts don't ambush me anymore
Don't force self-loathing to the fore
Worry and hope, contented side by side
Maybe arriving at a future time.

Stay or Stray

Do I want a sense of hopelessness or the false hope of
senselessness?

Violence at home, the sanctuary at work, the peace of resolution
looking less and less

The inner voice is distant now, a faint whisper tempting me to stray

To an empty, timeless world with neither tomorrow nor today.

My easily resistible force fails against the immovable object again
and again

Tiptoeing for a quiet life, recording my frustrations with a pen.

My family depends on me to deliver them from this hell

Temptations screaming for me to now to retreat into its shell

Dilemmas surround me; what's the right thing to do

Can I save the whole herd and the Black sheep too

The Black sheep strays to his own special grass

In his own solitude, watching real life pass.

Temptation goes silent when I have some kind of plan

When I have the confidence to do what I know, I can

I'm listless now with no clear direction to turn

Giving fuel to the fire for it to constantly burn.

Despair

Snatches of life,

remnants remain,

thoughts drowning in life's last waters.

Piercing regrets,

inflicted pain

aimed at your sons and daughters.

No crucifix,

nor candle burn

To ease passage across the Styx

An erroneous road

Mistaken turn

Collateral damage you could not fix.

Hate to Wake

Dawn breaks, fear rises

What will today bring

Enemies in friend disguises

I can't trust anything

Pressure rises inside my brain

Feelings screaming to get out

Can't face all this again

And a whisper becomes a shout.

Sensitivity awakes, emotions agitate,

I can't tell what they are

Fear surges, then evolves to hate

Pushing anger way too far

Simply Life

Not complicated; a simple short reality

Full of small pieces that are simple alone

Our minds merge them to build anxiety

Creating sins for which we must atone

Do unto others while improving your lot

Guide your goals around the impediments

Failures embraced, considered, then forgot

The far side of the grave is the place to repent.

Paranoia (the truth lies to me)

Do I walk on water so I do not make a wave

Only making small ripples, unable to be brave?

Second guessing the emotions, excusing the extremes

Reinforcing my culpability, eroding my self-esteem

Brightness appears sporadically, piercing the laborious gloom

Doubtless, peace will only come when a corpse lines a tomb

Push too hard, and Hell might reign fleetingly but cruelly,

Or tiptoe for eternity in Purgatories pointless duel

Trepidation covers every path leading to the lair

Paranoia fuelled fear anticipating whatever lies in there

Dealing with the facts should help, but the truth tells lies to me,

again and again ashamedly until I set the guilty free

Pain

Perpetual discomfort incessantly requiring respite

Annoyingly needy especially demanding at night

Intolerable at times whilst at others pretends it has fled

Nagging your mind until you crave the sleep of the dead.

Joy

Joining with others, celebrating outside the comfort zone

Oblivious to uneasiness, ecstatic you're no longer alone

Yet finding solace, you can return anytime to be on your own

Rain

Dampening your mood like a gargoyle on a carousel

Assaulting your ears with insistent echoes of its death knell

Blurring your vision and casting the scene in a sickly grey.

Overstaying its welcome, banishing all inside, keeping company
away.

Dependency

So hard to believe it took such a hold,

That could not have been me.

Episodes forgotten, I need to be told,

Addiction was too close to let me see.

Dependency lived in a cul de sac,

Where I'd go to be alone.

Hidden away with the wall at my back,

All the fruitless seeds being sown.

Vodka the vehicle, blind before I leap,

Jumped to escape my mind.

Blunted thoughts can't cut very deep

Redemption too dark to find.

Conclusion

I hope you enjoyed reading this collection of poems and thoughts and if needed was of some help to you. This has been a long journey for me, and I have reached a place in my life where I am content. There are still ups and downs, but my default mood is a good place to be.

If you have any comments, criticisms, or questions you can contact me at conorrichardson@gmail.com

Milton Keynes UK
Ingram Content Group UK Ltd.
UKHW020830280723
425958UK00016B/606